Good Times with Gregory

Birds: Rescuing a Baby Bird

Written by: Helen J. Davis (Grandma Davis)

Illustrated by: Robyn L. Davis

This is My Book:

....

Dedication

This book is dedicated to
all children
who are separated from those they love.

May God watch over you and bless your life
until those who love you
are reunited with you once again.

Publisher:
Whitehall Publishing, PO Box 548, Yellville, AR 72687

ISBN# 978-1-935122-10-4
$12.95 US

Ding, dong.

You came back!

Yes, no matter how far, wherever you are, I will always come back to you.

I love you, Grandma.

I love you, Gregory.

Are you ready for our adventure?

Yes, what are we going to do today?

We need to hurry. I saw something on the way here that I want you to see.

What?

Come quickly.

Grandma, you sound so serious, is there a problem?

Oh yes, Gregory, a matter of life and death.

Life and death? *Wow.*

Ok, we are here.

What? I don't see anything.

Stop. Look down.

Eww --- what is that?

It's a baby bird. A very, very little baby bird.
It's called a hatchling.

But, Grandma, it doesn't have any *feathers.*

I know. That's why it's called a hatchling. It's probably less
than a week old. See how it has its eyes closed?

Hatchlings don't usually
open their eyes. Pretty soon
it will open its eyes and it
will be called a nestling.
Then it will start to get feathers.

Hatchlings and nestlings
do not have any feathers.

Wow. What's it doing on the ground?

It probably fell out of the nest.

Fell?

Yes. Some people think that the parents push the weak birds out of the nest and that's why some hatchlings and nestlings end up on the ground. That's simply not true. Mother and Father birds are very careful about their children. They care for them and would never intentionally push one of their children out of the nest.

Oh, so it fell? Why don't they put it back?

They can't. They don't have any arms to pick it up. They could grab it with their beak much like a tiger picks up his baby cubs with his teeth, but the bird's pointed beak would hurt the baby.

Also, the parent birds don't have enough strength and control in their beaks to pick up the bird.

What happens if the hatchling doesn't get back into the nest?

Well, the hatchling does not have any feathers so it has a hard time regulating its body temperature. If the hatchling doesn't get back into the nest where the nest can protect him and the parents can keep him warm and feed him, he will die.

I wouldn't want that to happen.

No, Gregory. Neither of us would want that to happen.

What do you do if the bird is on the ground but it has feathers?

You should do nothing. Step aside and watch. Watch for the parents to come back. When a bird has its feathers, it is called a fledgling. A fledgling spends its day learning to fly and to take care of itself. If it is out of the nest, it is in training. They can be fun to watch at this age, but don't touch them.

Are they safe on the ground?

Sometimes. You just really need to be observant before you do anything. When birds have babies, the parents are always nearby either watching or gathering food to feed their babies or training it to fend for itself.

Is it alive?

Yes, dear. See how his stomach is moving in and out? Just like yours. Put your hand on your stomach right here. See how your hand is moving out from your body and then in towards your body? You are breathing air in and filling up your lungs and your diaphragm just like the baby bird.

How will it get back into the nest?

That's where we come in. We need to help him get back into his nest.

How are we going to do that?

We need to pick him up very gently and put him back in the nest.

Won't the parents get mad at us for touching the baby?

You know, Gregory, a lot of people think that but it is not true. Some people think that the parents will reject the baby because the parents can smell the human that touched the baby bird. Birds have a very bad sense of smell.

Unless they see you touching their baby they probably won't know that you touched the baby.

So can I put him back in the nest?

Certainly. How do you plan to do that?

Well, when my sister was little her neck wasn't very strong so I think I should probably slide my hand under the entire body so that nothing bends or breaks.

That's good thinking, Gregory. I'm proud of you.

Ok, so now?

Well, after you get him in your hand, where are you going to put him?

Oh, the nest! We need to find the nest.

Yes. Let's not pick him up until we find the nest.

Grandma Davis and Gregory look up
and all around to try and find the nest!

Grandma! I think I found it! Look!

Hmm ... it's pretty far up there. Over my head and well over yours.

What are we going to do? If we can't put him back in his nest he'll die, won't he?

Maybe we should just take him home with us.

No, Gregory. We should never take a wild animal home from his habitat.

What's a habitat?

A habitat is a fancy word that means where something lives.

A fish lives in water. Water is a fish's habitat.

Oh, so my house and my neighborhood would be my habitat?

Yes. You are very smart, Gregory.

Grandma?

Yes?

**Why did you call the bird wild?
Birds are not wild.**

Saying that something
is wild means that they
live in the "wild."
Now, realistically,
this patch of trees is
not what anyone would
call wild.

But in Science, we use the word "wild" to describe anything that is
not controlled by humans. Humans can't control how these birds
live or what they do to their habitats so we call this "wild."

Grandma, is the patch of trees behind my house "wild?"

Yes, technically it would be considered wild.

Cool.

What are we going to do, Gregory? We need to get this bird back in his nest so his parents can take care of him.

And soon, Grandma.
We need to hurry.

Let's think. It's better to think and plan before you do anything than to just do something and then find out you cannot do what you thought you could do.

Ok.

We have found the nest. It's high above our heads. We need to get to the nest, but how?

Grandma Davis and Gregory
take a minute to think!

**Grandma, I could climb the tree.
I could get close to the nest.**

But, can you climb the tree with only one hand while carefully protecting the baby bird with your other hand?

Hmmm ... I could try.

It's really not safe.

Is there a safer way to get up there?

Grandma? Are you very strong?

Well, I take my vitamins every day. I exercise. I eat good foods. I don't smoke, drink, or take drugs.

I do all those good things, too.

It's good that you take care of yourself. It's important to do that all of your life.

I'm so happy that you take care of yourself. That means we will have lots of times to visit because you will be around and healthy a long time.

Why did you ask if I was strong?

Well, I was thinking that I could climb on your shoulders and that would get me close to the nest.

Well, we could try that.

Gregory carefully climbs onto a rock --
-- then onto Grandma Davis' shoulders.

Ok. Stretch!

Can you reach the nest?

Oh, Grandma! There's an egg in here and two other babies!

The parents are probably close so don't touch anything.

They've probably been watching us this whole time.

Gregory carefully looks around to see if the parents are nearby.

Grandma, this is a really pretty egg.

What's it look like?

It's brown with black speckles.

Oh, these must be baby cardinals. That must be a cardinal nest.

How do you know that?

The egg of the Northern Cardinal is brown with black speckles.

Look over there!

See that very pretty bird that's mostly red? That's probably the baby's father. The mother is probably here somewhere, too. She's a little harder to spot because she camouflages with the trees.

What's camouflage?

Camouflage is a big word that means blends in with the background. Look at your shirt. What color is it?

Brown.

Now, get off my shoulders and stand by that tree.

Look, Grandma! I'm the same color as the tree!

Yes, Gregory. You are camouflaged.

That's pretty cool.

So the mom is probably brown?

Yes. She's brown with just a little bit of red on her head.

I think I see her.

She's right there.

Why aren't the mom and dad together?

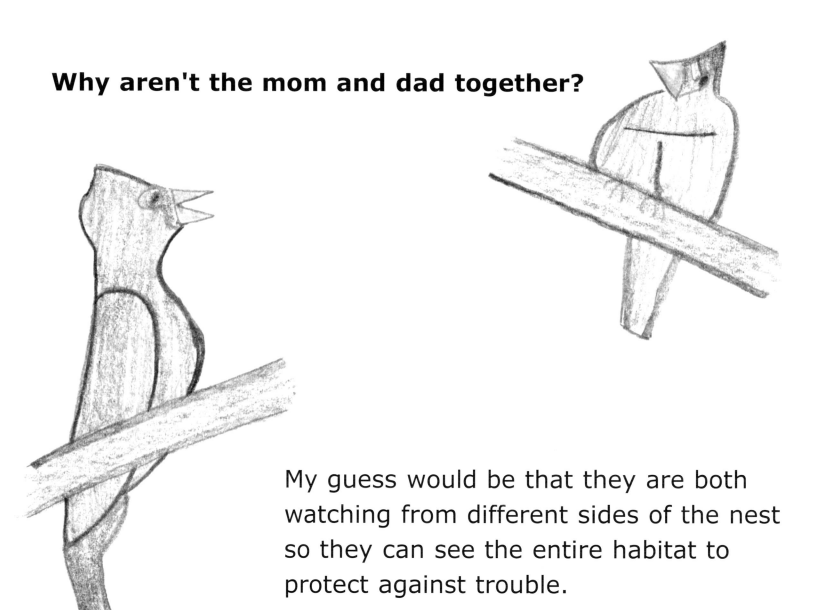

My guess would be that they are both watching from different sides of the nest so they can see the entire habitat to protect against trouble.

Well, are you ready to put this baby back in the nest?

Yes.

Ok. Carefully scoop him up.

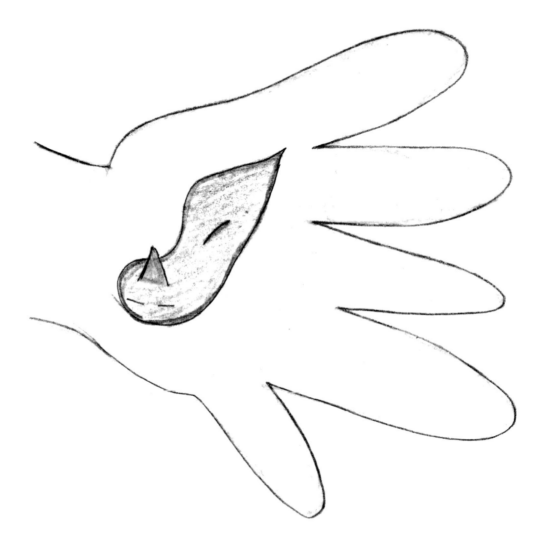

Gregory gently picks up the baby bird in his hand.

Climb onto that rock, then carefully onto my shoulders.
Now, slowly. Slowly.

Gregory climbs onto Grandma Davis' shoulders.

I am at the nest. I'm putting him in the nest right next to the egg. Goodbye little baby. Get well. Be strong. Come and visit me sometime.

Gregory, that was very responsible of you. You were very calm and very careful with that baby.

You probably saved his life. I am so proud of you.

I feel really good about helping the baby bird. Do you think his parents will come and help him now?

Yes, Gregory.

Did you want to stay and watch for a little while?

Could we?

Sure. We have a few more minutes.

Grandma, why is the dad a bright red but the mom is a dark brown?

There are probably a couple of reasons. Since the mom stays with the children a lot while the dad is off getting food, she needs to camouflage more to hide from any predators.

What's a predator?

Another big word today, huh? Predators are living things that eat other things. Cats eat mice. The cat would be a predator of a mouse.

I see.

What's the other reason?

Well, almost all male birds are brighter colored and fancier looking than female birds.

This is so that male birds can attract the attention of female birds.

Then male birds and female birds will be able to get together and have baby birds.

It only can happen if the females notice the males.

Look, Grandma! The parents are back at the nest!

Oh, good. You were successful in bringing the family back together. The hatchling will be fine now.

I understand a lot about baby birds now, Grandma, and all those new big words.

I'm glad.

It's time we need to be heading back to your home now.

Grandma Davis and Gregory walk home silently hand-in-hand thinking about today's big adventure.

I feel sad, Grandma.

I feel sad, too.

It's okay to feel sad.

I think about you when you aren't here.

No matter how far or how long life takes me away from you, I am always thinking about you.

I try to remember all the things we have done together.

Me too. I really enjoy my time with you.

I'm glad when we can get together.

I am, too.

Grandma Davis walks
Gregory to his door.

When will I see you again?

I don't know. Hopefully not too long.

That makes me sad, too.

Me too. Until we see each other again, we can pretend we are standing right with each other sharing the time together whenever we see a baby bird flying.

You know Jesus will be with you until we see each other again.

I know.

He will help you to feel better when you are sad.

I know.

Grandma? Does Jesus stay with you, too?

Yes, Gregory. Until I see you again, Jesus will stay with me and help me feel better too.

He loves you and He loves me.

He will be with you and He will be with me until we are together again.

I love you, Grandma.

I love you, Gregory.

Grandma Davis leans down and whispers...

Until next time.

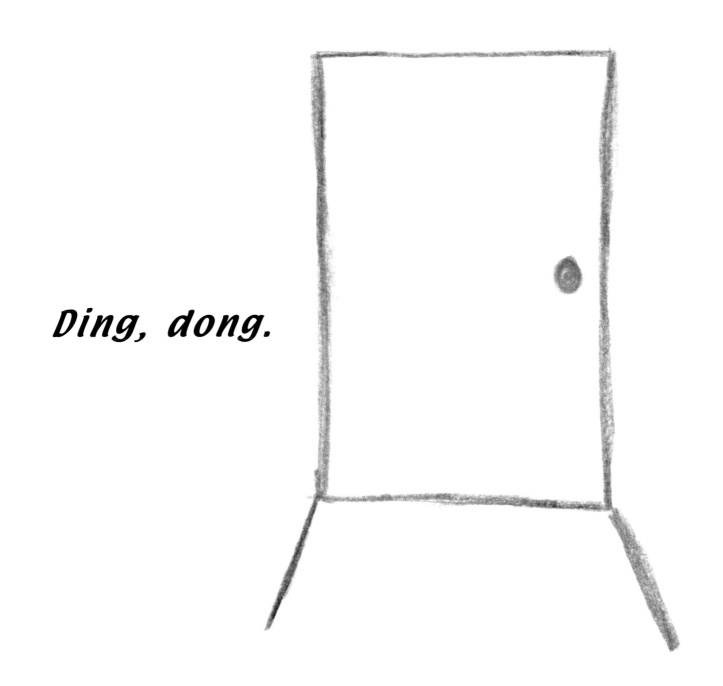

Ding, dong.

Order Page

Share more Good Times With Gregory by ordering all the books in the series!
To order on-line, visit www.GrandmaDavis.com.

Quantity			Total
_____	Good Times with Gregory, *Airplanes: A Visit to a 747*	$12.95	_____
_____	Good Times with Gregory, *Birds: Rescuing a Baby Bird*	$12.95	_____
_____	Good Times with Gregory, *Construction: Big Machines & Their Uses*	$12.95	_____
_____	Good Times with Gregory, *Deafness: Using American Sign Language*	$12.95	_____
_____	Good Times with Gregory, *Elephants: A Trip to the Zoo*	$12.95	_____
_____	Good Times with Gregory, *Food: Fun in the Kitchen*	$12.95	_____
_____	Good Times with Gregory, *Gardens: Playing in the Dirt*	$12.95	_____
_____	Good Times with Gregory, *Horses: A Visit to a Horse Farm*	$12.95	_____

Payment :
_____ American Express
_____ Discover Card
_____ Master Card/VISA
_____ Money Order/Check (make payable to Grandma Davis)

Shipping & Handling ($1.50 per book) _____

Order Total _____

Card Number: _____ **Expiration Date:** _____ **CCV Code:** _____
Signature: _____
Name: _____ **Ship To Address:** _____
City: _____ **State/Zip:** _____

Mail your order to: *Grandma Davis*, PO Box 369, Dublin, OH 43017
If you would like Grandma Davis to autograph any of your books (at no additional cost),
please provide specific instructions on the back of this form.

For more reading about Birds:
These are web sites Grandma Davis read through for some of the information she used when she wrote this book. Please have a
responsible adult help you to read through these web sites so you can find out much more information about birds and how they live.
http://www.mbr-pwrc.usgs.gov/id/framlst/i5930id.html
http://wildliferescue.ws/rehabilitation/baby_bird/
http://www.libertywildlife.org/urgent_wildlifeissues.html